```
PT 2625 .A44 Z857 c. 1
Stern, J. P.
Thomas Mann
```

Thomas Mann

by J. P. STERN

 *Columbia University Press*
NEW YORK & LONDON 1967

CARROLL COLLEGE LIBRARY
HELENA,

COLUMBIA ESSAYS ON MODERN WRITERS is a series of critical studies of English, Continental, and other writers whose works are of contemporary artistic and intellectual significance.

Editor: William York Tindall

Advisory Editors

Jacques Barzun   W. T. H. Jackson   Joseph A. Mazzeo   Justin O'Brien

Thomas Mann is Number 24 of the series.

J. P. STERN is a Fellow of St. John's College and a Lecturer in German at the University of Cambridge. He is the author of *Ernst Jünger: A Writer of Our Time; Lichtenberg: A Doctrine of Scattered Occasions,* and *Re-Interpretations: Seven Studies in Nineteenth-Century German Literature.*

Copyright © 1967 Columbia University Press
Library of Congress Catalog Card Number: 67–16891
Printed in the United States of America

Passages from the works of Thomas Mann are quoted, in the author's own translation, through the kind permission of Alfred A. Knopf, Inc., publishers of the authorized translation of Mann's works.

Thomas Mann

In the ten years that have passed since Thomas Mann's death his literary reputation has not had an easy time. The ideas which inform his novels and *novelle* are dismissed as being irrelevant to our present concerns, the subtle ironies of his styles and the intricacies of his narrative structures are said to founder in an excessive literary self-consciousness, demanding elaborate study rather than giving spontaneous pleasure. A recent critic has called him "irresponsible" and "an insidious . . . force for evil," and others, less extravagantly, have questioned the genuineness of the values intimated in his writings. Excessive or outdated intellectualism on one hand, esoteric formalism on the other—these, broadly speaking, are the present charges against him.

They are both plausible and misleading. Plausible, because Mann's concern with "ideas" is indeed more marked than that of any other modern European novelist, so that on occasion he does not scruple to present living characters as determined by the intellectual convictions they more or less clearly profess, or by the current of ideas to which they more or less consciously react. The charges turn out to be misleading as soon as we realize that there is nothing inadvertent or "abstract" about the patterns of Mann's stories, that the interplay of "ideas" and life is an integral part of his fiction: in the form of this interplay he saw life, here above all lies the distinctness of his art. That the "ideas" are present in a way in which they are not in the work of a Henry James is obvious enough; certainly, T. S. Eliot's

[3]

tribute to James—"A mind so fine that no idea could violate it" —does not apply to Mann. The violation of a mind by an idea, on the other hand, may well serve as a definition of one of Mann's central themes; and intellectualism, not as the novelist's failing but as a motif of his narrative, as a thing hostile to life, is another.

Like the work of every great artist, Thomas Mann's writings challenge established critical preconceptions. The distinction between creativeness and criticism loses much of its force in a work which is itself (in Matthew Arnold's phrase) quite manifestly a "criticism of life." He is one of the few novelists of our age—André Gide is another—whose major works were written with the full and explicit cooperation of his *critical* intelligence. For him, creation is itself partly a critical act, a scrutinizing of the values by which the world—it is, I believe, still *our* world —lives, a questioning of what is valuable in experience and true to its facts. Consequently the heroes of his tales are often men and women who, from their station in life and their limited point of view, contribute to that criticism and scrutiny of values which is his own preoccupation. One may, on occasion, wish he would be more self-effacing. But, seeing that modern men are as often intellectuals as they are gamekeepers or bull-fighters, Mann's preoccupation is, after all, hardly very esoteric.

When Thomas Mann's *Buddenbrooks* appeared in 1901 he was twenty-six years old; not even the blandest of weekly reviewers could have called the two-volume work "a first novel of promise," for the simple reason that here all, or almost all, is achievement. (Forty-three years later in his Californian emigration Mann was moved to hear his friend Franz Werfel describe the work as "an immortal masterpiece": "I wonder," Mann then wrote, "whether it is not this book which, among all my works, is destined to last.") Its subtitle is "The Decline of a Family";

[4]

its setting, not named, is the patrician world of the Free City of Lübeck into which Mann himself was born and in which he grew up. Like several other stories, the novel reflects Mann's own mixed parentage (his father, a Senator, came from Hanseatic stock while his mother was born in Brazil of a part German, part Creole family); and the family whose life over three and a half generations he describes closely resembles his own. This unsparing or embarrassing (it depends on one's point of view) use of autobiographical elements is characteristic of much of his fiction, and so is his use of historical and scientific data and philosophical theories: to the traditional realism of social circumstance he adds the realism of knowledge.

The Buddenbrooks begin as rich shippers and corn brokers. The story opens around 1835, takes us through the abortive revolution of 1848, and ends some thirty years later. In the course of it the fortunes of "the Firm" rise to their highest peak of prosperity and thence catastrophically decline. Several disastrous marriages, a physical exhaustion in the family strain, one or two imprudent business transactions—these are the "effective causes" of the decline, causes such as we know them from the tradition of the realistic *romanciers*. And the exquisite, leisurely details in which Mann describes them—a piece of precise physical characterization here, an affectionately and ironically evoked episode there, an occasional scene of ribald humor aimed at a piece of ineptitude, or again the melancholy resignation of disappointed hopes, set out against a background of fine old silver and china and sumptuous dinner parties—all this makes the "effective causes" of that decline into a rich and varied spectacle of life. So much so that instead of asking *why*, we delight in the contemplation *that* it should be so. The young novelist's achievement is all the more remarkable if we bear in mind that Mann has no indigenous tradition to draw on; except for the Berlin novelist Theodor Fontane (to whom in the early

[5]

1920s Mann paid generous tribute), German literature has nothing to compare with the social realism of the English, French, or Russian novelists of the nineteenth century.

We proceed through the novel in an orderly way: from Johann Buddenbrook the Elder, all shrewd businessman and driver of hard bargains, to Jean the first Consul; hence to Thomas, the novel's central character, so much less firm in his decisions and health than his predecessors, frequently in need of comfort from heavy Russian cigarettes and of revivification from eau de cologne, with his beautiful but distant wife Gerda and his disarmingly silly sister Toni; and thence finally to Thomas's son Hanno who, after a muddled life of unending infections, awful school-reports, questionable friendships, and ecstatic improvisations on the senatorial grand piano, dies in a typhoid epidemic, aged fifteen. But as we proceed along this plane of action we become aware that not everything we witness belongs to the theme of decline. We notice, for instance, that there is in Jean a feeling of compassion and disinterested sympathy, which is stronger in him than it was in Johann the Elder; that in Thomas (Jean's son) compassion is joined by a strange and eventually unnerving capacity to think and feel himself into the minds of people, contact with whom is apt to impair his business sense; we come to understand why Thomas should be able to assert the old virtues of prudence, self-control, and hard work only vis-à-vis his brother Christian, a melancholy hypochondriac obsessed by an incontinent "artistic" passion for miming slightly off-color stories—a passion which Thomas understands only too well and which the older Buddenbrooks would have found most peculiar. By now we are hardly surprised when Thomas happens upon a book of pessimistic philosophy (it is Schopenhauer's) that speaks enticingly of death and the anonymous, timeless future waiting for "us" beyond the prison of our individuation, on the other shore;

and we find it no less convincing that in a moment of feverish insight, on the very margins of his ordinary existence, Thomas should fall under the spell of this philosophy and on the morrow, the spell having done its work, forget it all again. We notice that to his wife Gerda, Hanno Buddenbrook's beautiful mama, neither "the Firm" nor even the family means very much, and that the only thing which makes life tolerable for her is the violin. Here, then, there is something like a second theme, which stands in ironical (that is, hidden) contrast to the theme of decline, and which finds its completion in Hanno's musical precocity, in his sad little life that is draining away to the sound of erotically charged ingenious arpeggios and cleverly contrived modulations into minor keys.

The "effective causes" of the decline, we can now see, were not its "final causes." The theme of decline is counterpointed by the growth of a strange, problematic spirituality. Characters are shown to acquire an understanding and an empathy that eventually exceed their vital resources; others again possess artistic talents or aspirations that turn out to exceed their experience of life. Is it, then, this defective spirituality among the Buddenbrooks which we are to take as the "final" cause of the decline of family and firm? Thomas Mann doesn't say so. The realistic novelist leaves his reader to draw his own conclusion. Which is, that the full final cause is neither one (the commercial, social, and biological decline) nor the other (the growth of intellectuality and art in excess of life) but *this,* this very particular and living combination of both. And this conflict of forces which, in their isolation, are hostile to each other makes for the criticism of life. The criticism of the civilization that came to an end in August 1914, is no less profound for being transmuted into pure story. (Fontane, had he lived, would have been its best reader.) The mercantile ethos lacking in compassion, self-knowledge, and a sense of values beyond its vital and business interests versus spirituality and aestheticism lacking in and at last contemptuous of life itself—these are the story's protagonists; and they are also among the major causes of the European decline.

Thomas Mann's métier appears to absorb his every interest. Even his private letters slip easily into the tone of his public utterances, and these in turn are couched in the semiprivate tone of irony. In an undramatic, conscientious, almost pedantic way his was a life wholly devoted to his art, while his art was at all times deeply involved in the life of his native country; thus it was the art itself, rather than any political ambition, which drew him into the vortex of public events and ideological battles. When the First World War broke out he was living in Munich, since the 1850s the artistic center of Germany. He was now happily married to the daughter of a well-known German-Jewish family of financiers and scientists, with a growing family of highly gifted children, the renowned author of two novels, several exquisite *novelle*—among the finest examples of the genre in any language—a number of critical essays, and a melodramatic and overcharged play about Savonarola.

The war years put a temporary halt to Mann's fictional work. Like other German (and Austrian) writers he allowed himself to be absorbed by the national emergency, though he remained relatively unaffected by the national hysteria that seized most of his fellow-writers. The long essays written during the war, which include a remarkable study of Frederick the Great, were published in 1918 in a collection entitled *Betrachtungen eines Unpolitischen* (Meditations of a Nonpolitical Man). His partisanship—such as it was—of the German cause has often been attacked, though any condemnation of the book as war propaganda is largely nonsensical, if only because much of it was published *after* the cause he "served with his pen" was lost. The book is in search of a definition of Germany. The quality that gives it such doubtful value as war propaganda—the scrupulousness and unnerving truthfulness of the search—gives it also its lasting, indeed its literary, interest. We know that many of its views were already out of date by the time they were put down: the book speaks for a whole generation of German artists and intellectuals who, in asserting a self-consciously "nonpolitical" attitude, tried to salvage and validate the politics and ideology of the Second Reich in terms of an unworldly and spiritual conservatism. But then, the imagination of most novelists is "out of date" in the sense of being engrossed by a more or less distant past. The progressive, left-wing attitude of Thomas Mann's brother and fellow-writer Heinrich Mann, the antagonist in the dialectical arguments of the *Betrachtungen*, may well be a good deal more congenial to us, and Heinrich's opinions are certainly a good deal less ambiguous; yet in their commitment to, and advocacy of, a single, progressive point of view his opinions are a good deal less searching and therefore, to us, less interesting.

Great writers (as the East Germans found while Brecht lived in their midst) make uneasy political bedfellows. Certainly Thomas Mann understands this, and some of his argument is designed to secure for the "nonpolitical" writer the freedom from political commitment necessary for his work. Where Mann is less clear (and this unclarity he shares with many of Germany's greatest literary men) is in the recognition that his freedom, and indeed the "nonpolitical" attitude generally, is itself also a factor in a political situation. One's criticism of *Betrachtungen* is that, in a sense, the book does not take the analysis of the situation far enough, that its basic contradiction remains unresolved. It is concerned, in much of its argument, with the role of artists, writers, and intellectuals in German public life. Their views, and intellectual ideas generally, have

[9]

been taken a good deal more seriously in German public life than comparable views have been taken elsewhere; it is notorious that German political parties have invariably felt the need to call upon the support of philosophers and theoreticians of a more or less respectable kind. Thus the situation in which Mann's essays were written and which they analyze was such that their publication was bound to make a political impact—and the more telling the analysis the more lasting this impact would be. Yet (and this is the other side of the contradiction) *Betrachtungen* is anything but a political manifesto. It is the characteristic product of a writer who at all times (except in the period 1933–45) refused to commit himself to a cut-and-dried political message. The book is concerned with questions of the German national ethos, with Germany's foreign policy, with her conduct of the war with Russia, France, and Italy, with the problems of art and culture in the modern world, with the "German" alternative to the ideas of the French Revolution, with German literature and philosophy and the Lutheran religion, and, again and again, with German music and its function in the life of the nation. And upon all these questions it brings to bear that same complex and truthfully inconclusive and ironical attitude which in *Buddenbrooks* had yielded such remarkable illuminations of both characters and history. Yet for all that the book necessarily raised, and was made to fulfill, the expectation of a political message—after its complex and subtle antitheses had been blunted in the way that practical politics always blunts the subtle ideas of those who are more concerned with insight than with action. It is a dilemma which held an endless fascination for Mann. At the height of the Cold War (1955), introducing a collection of letters and last wills written by men and women condemned to death during the Second World War, he comments on the hopes for a new humanity expressed in these documents: "Was it all in vain? Their dream

[10]

and their death—all wasted? It cannot be so. No idea for which men of pure hearts have fought has ever perished from the face of the earth. Each one has attained reality—and, though in the process it takes on all the blemishes of reality, yet it gains life for itself."

No author can help having his thoughts corrupted. The difficulty here is that in *Betrachtungen* Mann's insight stopped short of a clear recognition that the meditations of the non-political man, however ironical and ambivalent, were in themselves liable to become an unequivocal political factor. The conservatism which the book ironically advocates is a high-minded and spiritual thing, it aims at preserving that *bürgerlich* attitude of mind from which had arisen some of the finest products of German culture. But practical politics is the sphere of association (often of the best under one common label with the worst), and it is therefore not surprising that, in spite of his many addresses in support of the new social democratic regime, Mann found himself quoted, well into the twenties, as one of the advocates of that "conservative revolution" whose ultimate aim was the destruction of the Weimar Republic.

One way *and* the other, most of Mann's political utterances are unfortunate. To say this is not to discount the great, heart-felt effort he put into them, the "commitment" they express. But what is he committed to? A generation earlier, and in an altogether simpler situation, Theodor Fontane confessed to a friend that "my preoccupation with politics was, after all, only a literary one." And this, when we have sifted the dialectics and heart-searchings of *Betrachtungen*, is true of Mann also. In his responsibility to the work of art lies the glory of the artist and the travail of the man. The *Betrachtungen*, as well as the many subsequent pronouncements on behalf of Weimar parliamentarian and social democracy, is, "after all, only" a trial ground for the arguments which inform Mann's works of

[11]

fiction, most obviously and immediately *The Magic Mountain*. With that in mind we may understand why the political argument is often so very personal in tone, and why the substance of the novel is so often couched in public, historical terms.

The Magic Mountain (1924), like *Buddenbrooks*, depicts the immediate past yet, by projecting that past and its dominant ideas into the present, gives an impression of contemporaneity. The novel spans seven years in the life of a "very ordinary young man" from the North-German plain, Hans Castorp by name, and ends in 1914, when its hero disappears into the muddy inferno of a battlefield in Flanders. The seven years, described with many ingenious variations of tempi, are Hans's years in a tuberculosis sanatorium above Davos, where he arrives "just for a short visit," to stay with his cousin who is one of the patients there.

The location, as well as the experiences recounted, is characteristic: the story is placed, all of it and quite explicitly, on the margins of ordinary human life, in a "hermetic" situation: the host who presides over this prolonged house party is death itself. Since his arrival, Hans Castorp has been in a febrile state of . . . mind? certainly of body. After a few days' stay he has a "thorough check-up" and is found to be suffering from a slight tubercular lesion. What could be more natural than that, having assured himself that his financial affairs in the "Flachland" will bear the strain, he should decide to stay on, for the cure. But once again we ask: is that the real reason? It all depends on what one takes to be a "real" reason. Hans, for instance, with his mixture of inertia and far from aimless curiosity, stays on even after it has become doubtful whether he is "really" ill—but then, even when his *petite tache humide* was first discovered he was told that most young men were at one time or another liable to the disease, at least in its latent form;

[12]

more dubious still, after a short time on the Magic Mountain Hans has read up enough medical information to know that high-altitude conditions are likely anyway to bring the latent disease to a head.

And this is what the Berghof sanatorium does: it brings that disease and many another to a crisis; it shows a whole range of emotions, mental attitudes, and ideological conflicts in their most acute, most "critical" form.

Of Hans Castorp's past in the "Flachland" we know two things: that he was a bright young naval engineer of good family, about to begin his career; and that several bereavements in his immediate family have left him with a little more than the "normal" awareness of the shadow that lies on all life. He is neither a bouncy extrovert nor a morbid melancholiac. He is an attractive young man with an abundant but ultimately not undiscriminating appetite—an appetite not for action but for knowledge-and-experience. He is intelligent but far from intellectual—indeed, one of the lessons he learns on the Magic Mountain is that intellectualism is as defective a way of life as mindless, irrational emotionalism. He *learns:* for his is a story of initiation, somewhat in the hallowed manner of the *Bildungsroman.* But with such moribund company and in such a febrile, overcharged atmosphere, is it not more likely to be a *parody* of those leisurely and circumspect tales of initiation in which nineteenth-century German novelists had described their heroes' journey into the good life? Here again Thomas Mann is recasting the boundary line of genres: creation and critical act merge, parody is to him not so much a humorous inversion of the original as a critique of it. Take this fragment from a conversation between Hans and Clavdia Chauchat, the Russian *femme fatale* with Kirghiz eyes to whom Hans is bound by a sympathy stronger than the tie of a single night of love; it begins with a request for a cigarette—

[13]

She stretched out her hand. "With those, at least, you are provided." She took a cigarette, negligently, from the silver case he held out to her. . . . Then he said: "Yes, I always have some. I am always provided, one must be. How should one get on without them? It's what is known as a passion, isn't it, when one is reduced to that. To tell the truth, I am not at all a passionate person, but I have my passions, phlegmatic ones." "I am extra-*or*dinarily relieved," she said, breathing out, as she spoke, the smoke she had inhaled, "to hear that you are not a passionate person. But how should you be? You would have to be different from the rest. Passionate—that means to live for the sake of living. But one knows that you all live for the sake of experience. Passion, that is self-forgetfulness. But what you all want is self-enrichment. *C'est ca.* You don't realize what revolting egoism it is, and that one day it will make you the enemies of the human race."

—and as the passage shifts from the personal and particular to the historical and general (from the singular familiar "du" to the plural), a good deal more than a critique of the *Bildungs-roman* and its solipsistic preoccupation with *Erlebnis* is accomplished. The shifts are subtle, the concrete narration is not disrupted; these people may not be "us," but they are of our flesh and blood; only occasionally, when looking up from the book, are we apt to wonder (as after a prolonged reading of Freud) whether any thing will ever again be just itself, just a cigarette or a pencil, mercifully meaningless, just a mere writing utensil.

The Magic Mountain is a story of initiation: into what? into life? But we are always *in* life, and so is Hans Castorp. How then can he expect to be initiated into it? Here again the location—Hans's experiences on the margins of life—is splendidly vindicated by the peculiarly experimental character of his seven years; which in its turn is contrasted with a conveyed sense of the absolute passing of time, irretrievable, anything but experimental.

What exactly does Hans do in those seven long-and-short years? He makes a number of friends, enters into a great many disputes and, when he has had enough of them, withdraws; he

[14]

becomes the cause of a duel; falls in love with Clavdia Chauchat, sees her leave, and somewhat fitfully waits for her return; reads a good many medical books, dabbles in Freudian psychology and in various natural and occult sciences; learns to ski and almost freezes to death in a snowstorm; discovers in himself a love of music; accompanies his cousin Lieutenant Joachim Ziemssen and a good many other people, not all of them very dignified, to death's door and sees them off . . . *The Magic Mountain* is, above all, a conversational novel, a work in which action is mostly replaced by talk about action. (Since all the inhabitants of the Berghof are *morituri*, it is hard to see how things could be otherwise.) Worse than that, the time that is not devoted to talk is taken up by vast meals, macabre promiscuity, a tragicomic duel and two suicides (as if the "normal" rate of demise weren't high enough), and by the kind of entertainments that sick people devise for themselves with the help of those who make a living from their sickness—a sickness unto death for most, and salvation there is none. For, worst of all, the question of what the lesson of all those years is meant to yield is answered as ambiguously as was the question why exactly Hans remained in that hothouse amidst the snowy peaks in the first place. Of course, the long conversations and the "morbid" action are all part of the marginal situation in which the novel is placed and which it is designed to illuminate; but why place it in that situation? what is the author's end that he should make it so difficult of attainment?

As a matter of literary fact, the impression the novel leaves with us is the opposite of morbidity and boredom. The sense of irony and humor which enlivens the story almost everywhere (it does have its *longueurs* too) isn't exactly of the homely kind, and some of it is pretty black. Yet it is not a sick humor but rather humor *about* sickness, and thus a liberation; *about* chaos and decay, and thus a harbinger of order and life;

[15]

about the indignities of death, and thus a brave rebuttal of all the existential blather about death's majesty. The style of the novel, elaborate and finicky and curiously pedantic even while it describes physical decay and the corruption of souls, is in firm and deliberate contrast with its subject matter. And the humor arises where style and one's expectations about the subject matter clash. Thus men and women who are mortally ill claim to have more wisdom than "the stupid, healthy people down below," yet are made silly by accidie and the terror of death; a mixture of spirituality and national bolshevism is preached by an inquisitorial maniac (many of whose views were Thomas Mann's own, in the *Betrachtungen*); accurate insights into human motives are vouchsafed to people who haven't enough life left to act on them yet claim a special nobility for their disablement; and love itself, the most life-giving of the passions, is now heightened now dispossessed by the proximity of death.

Whatever Hans Castorp is to learn from his protracted sojourn, it is unlikely to be a tag. The initiation into life is itself a piece of life, it will not yield an unambiguous precept: Do this —avoid that. And the lesson that death, Hans's grim host, teaches him? What Hans learns in a dream during a snowstorm on that skiing expedition from which he almost doesn't return is that the untrammeled dominion of death over men is as corrupting to their minds and hearts as is the frivolous avoidance of all thought of death. To allow life to be informed but not paralyzed by the apprehension of disease and the expectation of death—to strive for a refinement of life through an intelligent knowledge and experience of life's enemies: that is the vision which (again, only briefly and unsteadily and on the margins of life) opens up before Hans. Whether he can live up to it is another story.

The Marxist critic Georg Lukács (who himself makes a far

from flattering appearance as that inquisitorial Jewish Jesuit)
has pointed to the historical symbolism that lurks behind many
figures and arguments in the novel. Thomas Mann himself, in
a lecture at Princeton in May 1939, underlined its critical and
European dimension, pointing out (surely an act of supereroga-
tion) that its characters embody a great many of those
political, social, and philosophical ideas which came to a head
in the fateful summer of 1914. When he began writing it, in
1912, *The Magic Mountain* was to be a short novella, built
round the visit of an impressionable young man to a sanatorium;
when he finished it, twelve years later, it had grown into a
panorama of modern Europe. And it speaks for his art even if it
does not speak for human nature that no opinion expressed in
the novel is so absurd that it was not in fact seriously defended
in the Europe of that age by some intellectual aesthete or cave-
man. Yet the young hero is never lost sight of. It is as much for
his sake as for the sake of the critique that the "ideological
fighting-cocks and pedagogic prattlers" round him (shades of
Lukács, but also of Thomas and Heinrich Mann) conduct their
disputations; for, as Hans says in his dream, "Man is master
over the opposites" of life and death, and not only over these.
And here lies the fullest meaning of the "message" of the novel,
in this recognition that ideology and ism and dialectics are not
enough, that the *Gegensätze* on which European intellectuals
and politicians had been reared and for the sake of which they
had gone to war were a lethal chimera. A tag after all? To
those who have never experienced or even contemplated the
spell of ideological commitment it may look as though the
Magic Mountain has given birth to nothing better than a com-
monplace mouse. "The subject is not exhausted in its conclusion
but in the working out of it; nor is the result attained the real
whole, but it and the process of arriving at it," says the gnomic
Hegel. Thomas Mann's characteristic truthfulness, as well as

[17]

the real value of his insight, lies not in a detachable message but in the weight of the odds against which the insight is achieved, in the imaged and full presentation of the case for the other side.

Hans Castorp, with all his engaging modesty, occasional exasperation, and consistent good humor, is an enormously important person. He is the heir apparent of the European cockpit, it is he who will have to live in it. Or will he? At the end of the novel the two planes, the personal and the historical, intersect. The penultimate chapter, in which the national and ideological antagonisms among the inmates gather momentum, is called "The Great Irritation." Then follows "The Roll of Thunder." General mobilization is declared in Germany, Hans abruptly leaves, and the last glimpse we have of him is through a barrage of shells and heavy machine gun fire, ducking in the mud and, Schubert's "Lindenbaum" on his lips, advancing on the enemy.

Is that the lesson he has learned? the end to which he undertook that strenuous journey of initiation? we ask in some bewilderment. It is. Certainly Hans's was a special case, special in Aristotle's sense of "eminently good of its kind," and therefore representative, which is why his story was eminently worth telling. But he was not so special that he should be exempt from the logic of events—events, too, let loose by the very ideas he had contemplated on the Magic Mountain. We might well prefer him to conclude his "initiation" and "cure" of his own free will rather than by following the trumpet call of the Fatherland, but—"du réalisme avant tout." The call was sounded, and it ill behooves us, by confusing 1914 with 1939, to doubt that Hans could obey it with a good conscience and a noble hope in his heart. It is possible though not very likely, the author tells us as he bids him farewell, that he may survive the slaughter; and then put into practice that knowledge-and-experience,

[18]

that critical and intelligent love of life he acquired in his seven years on the mountain. But come what may it has been *his* story, an experiment yet a thing irretrievable, an initiation *and* a life; the rest is in the lap of the gods.

"The artist and society"—one scans the phrase with a sinking feeling, it has suffered overexposure by the critics. Long before *Buddenbrooks*, Thomas Mann's literary work begins, in the 1890s, with short stories that center on the relationship between the sensitive or artistic man and "the world" around him that shows no understanding of his gifts and very little sympathy for the deprivations that go with those gifts. Many of Mann's greatest *novelle* belong quite explicitly to this theme: *Tristan* (1903), from which grew *The Magic Mountain; Tonio Kröger* (of the same year) and *Death in Venice* (1912), his two most famous stories. Indeed, there is no major work, hardly an essay or sketch, hardly even a letter, in which the topic does not receive his ever-renewed attention. Many a reader has been put off by what he has felt to be a self-conscious and esoteric pre-occupation, and some critics have not made things easier by insisting that Thomas Mann should be seen above all as "an artist's artist," that "the mediation of art" is his paramount concern. It may well be true (a discouraged reader will argue) that the claims of art are at odds with the claims of ordinary morality; that (as Nietzsche was not the first to remark) poets are liars; that the "putting on ice" of personal feelings is, as Tonio Kröger says, the precondition of artistic success; that some of the greatest achievements of modern art are the off-spring of decadence; that the discipline which informs an art-ist's style is more properly the place to seek for an intimation of his moral worth than are the opinions expressed in the work; and that the intricacies, even the most technical, of the craft of letters are of consuming interest . . . : but are these matters that ought to go into a fictional story? What authentic concern are they of ours who are not artists? Is not this indulgence in "artistic" themes, this aesthetic circle, itself a sign of decadence?

There is little doubt that these artist stories owe their great success and fame in the first instance to a public that felt flattered at being in the know, at being taken (sometimes quite literally) behind the scenes. But their more permanent value emerges wherever the aesthetic circle is breached, wherever "art" or "literature" is used also as a symbol for the creative activity of the human spirit in its more varied aspects. Art, then, is seen as a mission and a fate. It is achieved at the cost of a personal or emotional sacrifice. Its end is illumination and delight, but it is a profoundly uneconomic activity—the means are apt to seem vastly in excess of the end. Often, when exploring this theme, Thomas Mann tends to stress the gulf between means and end, art and life, thus making it difficult for art to function as a symbol. But in doing so he is not acquiescing in the separation of life from the things of the spirit, but criticizing that separation and pointing to the impoverishment it entails. In *Tonio Kröger* those who have no inkling of art are idealized as blue-eyed, fair-haired enviable innocents, and the gulf between them and the knowing artist is not really bridged. (Curiously enough, the earlier *Buddenbrooks* had been wholly free from this sort of sentimentality.) In *Tristan* the hypersensitive hero, author of a few arty sketches, is reduced to a sterility only a little less ridiculous (because more vulnerable) than the brutish cheerfulness and bewildered jealousy of his antagonist, the owner (alas) of a sausage factory. In *Death in Venice*, on the other hand, the theme of the separation and ensuing decadence is taken so far, and treated so single-mindedly, that the living story it yields carries us beyond the esoteric restriction.

In the context of these artist stories Mann's passion for leit-motifs and symbolical correspondences enables him to breach

[20]

the aesthetic circle; happily it works in the direction not of literariness but life. Where "a pencil is never just a pencil" had on occasion resulted in a narrowingly literary effect, "art is more than just art" results in a liberation. *Death in Venice* is the story of the aging literary master who has spent a lifetime in the ever more exacting service of his craft. When the story opens, Gustav von Aschenbach is at the height of his fame. In a moment of spiritual and physical exhaustion he is exposed to the seduction of Eros and the blandishments of death. It seems poetically right that his agony should be consummated in Venice, that city of supreme artistry and artifice where Richard Wagner too had died, at the height of his fame and in surprising solitude: for just as Venice, so very obviously, "stands for" art, it is also a rich and ornate piece of life. Again Thomas Mann chooses a marginal situation—the passion of the erstwhile moralist for a beautiful boy—using this "scandalous" though unrequited relationship to clinch the corruption of the entire being of a man whose achievement, literary and existential, had risen from the ashes of self-denial. Aschenbach succumbs because, in a lifetime of "service to the spirit," he stifled within himself those "early precious tribulations of the heart" which are at war with morality and order. His knowledge of man (of himself) and hence his literary achievement were bought at less than the highest price. Now come corruption and collapse—but they are indistinguishable from the moment of delight *and* the last tremors of creativity. And beyond all this, enveloping almost the whole story, is Mann's ironical, elaborately circumstantial yet enigmatic style, the story's highly organized structure with its suggestive episodes, contrasting moods, and telling (occasionally too telling) images. Once again the material, intimating chaos, is conquered by the creative mind, and an ambiguous victory results.

This victory too is a part of the story: "The magisterial pose

[21]

of our style is lies and foolishness, our fame and high repute a farce," so Aschenbach in his mind addresses the boy Tadzio, to whom he has never spoken in the flesh. But his story gives the lie to the lie: for as the poet's psyche capitulates before Eros and Thanatos (the forces he had denied), the veil of irony drops, the full price of knowledge-and-experience is exacted: the climax of the story illuminates no longer merely an "aesthetic problem" but the human condition. The reader is left not merely with the picture of an aging potential homoerotic killed by a stroke on the lido of a plague-ridden Venice but with a parable on the text "Man cannot live by his will alone."

In all these prewar stories, then, the negative, disabling aspect of the artistic activity predominates. *Death in Venice* contains the fullest statement of the predicament. Form, the hallmark of the artist's achievement (we read there), is janus-faced, "moral and immoral at the same time: moral, in so far as it is the result and expression of rigorous discipline, immoral—yes, even hostile to morality—in that its very nature is indifferent to good and evil." But is even that true? Is "the result and expression of rigorous discipline" in and by itself moral? Is passionate intensity enough, regardless of its object?

Mario and the Magician (1929) is among the finest *novelle* Thomas Mann ever wrote; it obeys the rules of the genre by being centered round "a single extraordinary event" (as Goethe observed), and by exploring to the full the circumstances of that event. The story is set in a fashionable Italian seaside resort in the era of Mussolini. It is told in the first person by a cultured, sophisticated German intellectual, who continues his holiday with his wife and family at Torre di Venere after the foreign visitors' season is over. It all begins with the weather:

The heat was excessive . . . it was African: the power of the sun that shone down on us was frightful, relentless. . . . Do you like that sort of thing? For weeks on end? Of course, it is the South, it is

[22]

classical weather, the climate wherein the culture of mankind first came to flower, the sun of Homer, and all that. But after a while, you know, one can't help feeling a sort of leaden inertia come over one.

This torpid atmosphere is made more uncomfortable still by spiky hints and an occasional rudeness from a few chauvinistic Italians. Clearly, the thing to do is to pack one's bags and go home.

Into this mood comes Cavaliere Cipolla, a traveling magician and hypnotist, whose gala performance is attended by all Torre, including visitors and the native population. The narrator takes his family to the show for the same reason, or lack of reason, that made him stay on: listlessness, a curious fascination, an aimless, detached desire to see what will come next. The whole thing turns out to be something of a scandal. In a very few minutes it becomes clear that the show is a piece of cheap sensationalism, quite unsuitable for the children. But first, here is Cipolla himself:

He came on to the stage with a rapid step that expressed his eagerness to serve his audience and gave rise to the illusion that he had come a long way at the same pace to appear before them, whereas of course he had only been standing in the wings. His apparel supported this fiction of a sudden arrival. A man whose age it was hard to determine but by no means young, with a sharp, ravaged face, piercing eyes and a compressed mouth, a small black waxed moustache and a so-called imperial in the hollow between lip and chin, he was dressed in street clothes of a sort of complicated evening elegance. He wore a wide black sleeveless cloak with a velvet collar and a satin-lined shoulder cape which, since his arms were hampered [by a riding whip hidden under the cloak], he held together in front with his white-gloved hands. He had a white scarf round his neck, and a top hat with a curved brim sat at a rakish angle well down on his forehead. . . . Cipolla had in his whole appearance much of the historic type of mountebank and charlatan; his very clothes emphasized it, pretentious as they were, for in places they were pulled tight and in others fell in absurdly loose folds. Something was wrong with his figure, both fore and aft, which was to become plain later on. But I must emphasize that

[23]

there was not a trace of personal jocularity, let alone clownishness, in his pose, his expression, or his behavior.

The evening begins with a few card tricks, feats of arithmetical memory, and thought reading. Gradually the Italian public is drawn into the performance—first the simple fishermen of the place, a waiter or two, then some visitors, a solemn young gentleman from Rome. From thought reading Cipolla moves on to hypnotism, his real art, and now the macabre fun begins in earnest. The audience is only too ready to provide volunteers, people egg each other on to join the battle of wills, and Cipolla triumphs over them all. One is made to dance, another to perform complicated calculations on the blackboard, a third to tell his most private thoughts, a fourth impersonates his girl friend and implants a kiss on Cipolla's sweaty gray cheek. The pandemonium reaches its climax when the entire stage is filled with will-less performing marionettes, dancing, contorted, stuttering, all firmly held on the Magician's leading strings. An endless barrage of comments and explanations ("Parla benissimo," say the Italians admiringly), cracks of the whip, dirty gray torrents of smoke issuing from behind defective teeth, frequent recourse to a bottle on the table behind him—the *artiste* Cipolla is giving his all. And as the hold of his will on victims and audience increases (they are all under his spell now, including our skeptical, bemused narrator), so the tone of Cipolla's comments gradually changes from flattery and mockery and cajoling to veiled insults, ridicule, contempt, searing hostility, all the way to open derision and malevolent triumph. The triumph of the ugly, misshapen, and sinister charlatan is a triumph of the ravaging will over an audience composed of "normal," trusting, nonwilling people. For this is what their ravished wills are reduced to: all they can do is to will *not* to do what Cipolla wills them to do, and from "willing not to" (the narrator claims) it is but a short step to not willing at all.

[24]

I know of no single work in which the predicament of the European liberal mind in the grip of the demagogue's will is so accurately portrayed as in this novella. The whole complex relationship between the demagogue and the masses is here. They are linked in a strange nexus of mutual fear and mutual need. For not only are the masses the mindless, will-less victims of his will, but his defective being is in bondage to their subjection and obedience; the moment his will gives out they will destroy him. And the relationship that is here depicted embraces also the intellectuals and aesthetes who (to begin with, at any rate) are too bemused, too fascinated by the lurid spectacle to protest against it. The parallels with the Fascist situation, with the Germany of Hitler's mass meetings of the twenties, are left implied, the macabre cabaret is left to tell its own story, which is completed by an ending almost as convincing as it is horrifying.

These obvious parallels show once more that the nature of Mann's commitment to the realities of his age takes the form of insight rather than partisanship. Thomas Mann is not that languid narrator, that tacitly approving intellectual. Far from it. In many articles and open letters before 1933 and after he urged upon his fellow-countrymen and the world at large a firm stand against the dictators, at least those of the Right. But that, in the pantheon of literature, is after all less important than the delight and illumination he was able to create by exploring one of the most characteristic situations of our age. "The problem of the artist"—Mann's favorite theme—is not wholly abandoned, but what it expresses is no longer a private, aesthetic concern. While describing a personal fate, the story opens out into a political meaning. Where Gustav von Aschenbach's "rigorous discipline" of the will was presented as a positive value, Cipolla's no less intense devotion to his métier is shown to be a source of evil. Yet there is no facile condemna-

[25]

tion. As in all great literature, the full meaning of the implied moral judgment is inseparable from an intimate understanding of, and sympathy with, the thing condemned. It is a fellow-feeling that enables the artist Thomas Mann to enter into that figure of deprivation eked out by the "creative" will, the figure of the *artiste* Cavaliere Cipolla.

On January 30, 1933, Hitler accepted President Hindenburg's offer of the chancellorship. Ten days later Thomas Mann left for Holland on a lecture tour; he did not set foot on his native soil again until July, 1949. Throughout the twelve years of Hitler's rule, which Mann spent in Switzerland, southern France, and the United States, he was tireless in his condemnation of National Socialism and in his propaganda on behalf of "democracy of both kinds," western and eastern. Deprived of his German nationality, he became for a short time a Czechoslovak citizen, then American, finally Swiss. During his American sojourn he found himself the unofficial spokesman of the German emigrants in the West, a benevolent father-figure to many less successful fellow-writers and intellectuals, a representative of what during the Second World War was called "the other Germany"; yet he was realistic enough to discourage any attempt to form a government in exile, recognizing that any future settlement would have to be based upon an unconditional defeat of Germany. He did not live the "dark night of exile" (the phrase is Karl Marx's)—certainly not in the sense of material hardship. He traveled widely and found himself the recipient of many honors (he was awarded the Nobel Prize in 1929); he held a teaching post at Princeton; in the house he built near Los Angeles he assembled round him his large family and circle of friends. Yet a profound and anxious concern for the state of Germany and Europe never left him. It is voiced in his letters, broadcasts, and public pronouncements, it delayed the

[26]

completion of the *Joseph* tetralogy, it is imprinted on *Doctor Faustus*, his last great work. Nor did the end of the war in 1945 bring release. In 1949 his eldest son, the writer Klaus Mann, committed suicide. When, in June, 1952, Thomas Mann left America for good, the country was in the throes of the McCarthy era, and he felt as though he were reliving the situation of Germany in 1933. His few sympathetic references to the East German regime were met by some Western critics with bitter hostility and personal invective. There is a sense in which his active political stand after 1933 may be seen as the paying of an old debt—the debt of the erstwhile "nonpolitical man"; he paid dearly indeed. He died in Zurich on August 12, 1955, at the height of his fame, the last survivor of a generation of writers who, rooted in the Germany of the nineteenth century, belong to the Europe of our own, less securely accommodated age.

Joseph and His Brothers, begun in 1926 and completed in 1943, is implicitly related to the exigencies of that time in being Mann's tribute to the national life and religious spirit of the Jews in their darkest hour. The massive work is encompassed by the Old Testament's most laconic and most attractive story —the story of Jacob, his brother Esau, and his wives Leah and Rachel (Volume I); of Joseph and his brethren (II); of Joseph's life in Egypt (III); and of their great family reunion (IV)— "I am Joseph; doth my father yet live?" (Genesis 45:3). Not the least but the greatest tribute one can pay the work is to say that it exquisitely and movingly fills in the interstices of the biblical story—that no reader of the novel can ever return to Genesis, indeed to the Old Testament, without feeling how enriched the human substance of it has become. Of the immense and painstaking labor of reconstruction, buttressed by extensive study of biblical and archaeological scholarship, no perti-

[27]

nent judgment can here be given beyond saying that its diverse learned sources are wholly integrated in the work; the story itself, at all events, forms a seamless garment. The elaborate theo- or rather cosmological speculations, on the other hand, though necessary to the story, are more problematic.

Literary works based on historical facts or accepted myth invite—they certainly cannot avoid—comparison with the patterns from which they were taken. What, then, in this vast panoramic retelling of the fortunes of Jacob-Israel's family, constitutes an enrichment of the familiar story? First, and most successfully, the traditional task of the storyteller is accomplished: he connects, that is motivates, the discrete biblical episodes in human and psychological terms. (Thomas Mann himself speaks of the connecting of ancient myth with modern psychology, of religion with Freud.) Among the countless examples of such felicitous connections one may single out the affairs of Potiphar's sumptuous household: Joseph's quick rise to the position of highest trust, Potiphar's high intelligence, gentle wisdom, and impotence, his wife's passionate infatuation with the young and beautiful Hebrew servant and her hysterical denunciation of him, all culminating in the grand scene in the courtyard where, before the assembled household, Potiphar tries Joseph and, secretly aware of the falsehood of the accusation, with a show of great severity passes a most lenient sentence. But then, almost any human relationship—Jacob's with the crafty and dour Laban; Reuben's with his brethren, after they have thrown Joseph into the well and he has returned to find out whether their father's favorite is "quite dead"; or Joseph's with the young Pharaoh, "the dreamer" Amenhotep IV, who is more interested in the problems of monotheism on which his Chancellor can converse with such perfection than he is in the Chancellor's equally accomplished knowledge of agriculture and economics—any of the countless relationships on which the Bible touches only briefly (and others which it doesn't mention) offer the delight of a humanly motivated and richly imaged narration; and Jacob's first meeting with Rachel at the well, his love for his tender and brave young bride, and his sorrow when she dies in childbirth—these early scenes form perhaps the most moving part of the whole story.

On this simple narrative plane the tetralogy has a richness of life and a Tolstoyan abundance of characters, episodes, and concrete circumstance which are unique in Mann's entire work. But this is not, this cannot be, all: Mann is bound to inform the biblical story with a modern concern. And with the double theme that holds this narrative profusion together he returns to the preoccupation of a lifetime. He asks the age-old question: What is it in the characters of the members of this family, in the lives of their forebears, that made them chosen by God? What is the sign of their election? Why did He speak to Jacob on that fateful night at Bethel, why did He never speak to Esau or Laban? And to this question, which the Bible too asks, Thomas Mann gives two closely connected answers; they issue from the biblical argument, but they lead into a sphere that is alien to it.

The family sign of the election (so runs the first part of the answer) is a supreme quality of care—a deep, unsettling, unappeasable caring for spirituality and for a God, a worrying, "neurotic" concern for the right and godly way of life, a turning away from the enticements of the tangible world, a contempt for those who put their trust in a settled existence and its monuments of stone, the Pyramids. This spiritual sign Abraham had when he pondered on his God—when he all but created that God in the image of his own caring—and Jacob too, with his limp, when, in spite of his great prosperity and "miraculous" success as a sheep farmer, he packed up all his possessions and left Laban, his incensed father-in-law.

[29]

Nor is this existential care for God that Mann depicts to be equated with morality. Take the scene in which young Jacob, having by a fraud extracted the blessing from Isaac, his gullible and half-knowing blind father, runs away from home and on his inglorious flight is overtaken by his revengeful cousin, young Eliphas. What now ensues is a scene of sheer humiliation. Jacob simply grovels before the handsome, strong boy. He talks and talks in order to placate him. He cringes in the desert dust, kissing his feet, until Eliphas turns away in disgust from the undignified spectacle. Jacob will do anything—deny the fraud, put the blame on his mother, he will even belittle the significance of the blessing; every single piece of his possessions (except, incidentally, a ring which he carefully hid in his belt) he is prepared to part with. And he comes away from the encounter having lost all that men prize most dearly: his honor and good name, his courage and manliness, every shred of human dignity. Yet it is not just his bare life that he buys so dearly. For his is a special kind of life, which he knows to be worth more than all the decent sentiments and possessions that he cast down before the foolish warrior-boy: a life that he, Jacob, knows to be blessed, now and forever. He has stolen the blessing but it is *his*. Hungry, weary, the tears of fear and shame hardly dry on his cheeks, he walks by the side of his lame camel through the desert. He is on the very margins of life, his sense of humiliation will not allow him to seek out the company of men. He finds a circle of boulders and there lies down to sleep. And what he dreams is the dream of his life, which he will never forget. The dream discloses to him, for a brief night only, the knowledge of his God on Whom he will meditate and Whom he will serve in sorrow and care throughout his life, a knowledge of good and evil not as the world knows it. Or take again the story of the brethren's ghastly slaughter of the circumcised Shechem and his Canaanites, their revenge for the defilement of Dinah the daughter of Leah. All these events are presented as part of an essentially spiritual concern, to which the barbaric, "pagan" morality of the Canaanites, or the Egyptians, is irrelevant; the events are justified and become meaningful as part of God's design with His chosen people. And at the final reconciliation and reunion of the family in Egypt, their new home, the election for grace once again falls not on him who rose to highest office and greatest glory among the foreigners but on him who was ever the most troubled by his sins of the flesh, on him who, among them all, most deeply cared: it is Judah and not Joseph who receives the dying Jacob's last and most solemn blessing. This is why Joseph, although he dominates all but the first part of the story, is by no means its sole hero. He is certainly the most attractive and charming character Mann has ever created. The lucky and adventurous course of his life shapes much of the novel; on his character, the places in which he dwells, and the countless men he so easily befriends the narrator's richest imagination is lavished. And it may be said that in presenting Joseph as an artist in the medium of life Mann sees in him the concrete fulfillment of those aspirations toward a unity of art or spirit and world which the heroes of his artist stories had striven for in vain. But it is precisely because Joseph is so lucky and successful, because his very interest in the religion of his father and forebears is a worldly interest and not an anxious care—because, in brief, he is "the provider of bread"—that he is not the novel's hero in the fullest sense, and that he is not chosen.

While this mode of election through care takes its origin in the biblical story, the characters who display it have a family likeness with the earlier heroes of Thomas Mann's novels (as well as with his Doctor Faustus). Thomas Buddenbrook, Gustav von Aschenbach, even Hans Castorp were not the elect of the God of the Israelites, yet in their different circumstances

[31]

and ways they too were searching for the most strenuous, the most exacting deliverance. And the suggestion was present in those earlier works—it is present here—that the strenuousness of the search itself is the only intimation we can have of its validity. This is why, in the *Joseph* novel, the question of the truth of faith is never directly raised: the strenuous commitment to the spiritual is meant to intimate a positive answer. But at this point, where the high price of belief is made to stand as proof of the validity of belief, where (in Rilke's phrase) "the strenuous labor of the heart" is made to do service as an ontological proof, we leave biblical ground and enter on an existential preoccupation characteristic of German literature in the twentieth century.

In a work that ranges as freely and as playfully over aeons of time as do these volumes, it would be egregious to complain of anachronism. Thomas Mann playfully invites the charge only to rebut it. He constructs an ingenious scaffolding of symbolical cross-references, typological correspondences, and seachanges of time, to and fro across the books of the Old Testament and into the New, in order to contain the episodic profusion. Biblical exegesis from medieval times onwards has insisted on the essential continuity of the Judaic and Christian traditions, and has seen Christ and the Virgin Mary prefigured in certain characters of the Old Testament. So that here too the narrative mode of the novel appears to be anchored in religious orthodoxy: taking its origin in the biblical text, the novel appears to be fulfilling its expectation. But now the second half of the answer to the novel's central question begins to emerge, and this, alas, takes us far away from the Bible, into a literary desert.

To the storyteller's traditional task of connecting and motivating his episodes Thomas Mann adds a further device—he allows his characters to share in his task. Jacob, Joseph, Judah, Potiphar, and the young Pharaoh are all treated as historical

[32]

personages who lived at a certain time, but there are also moments in which their lives blend with those of their forefathers. (Eliezer, for instance, who is Jacob's oldest servant, talks to the young Joseph as though he had served Abraham too.) Moreover, they all have moments of consciousness that allow them to see themselves (and occasionally one another) as parts of a cosmic plan, a preordained whole. But the peculiar effect of this kind of knowledge is to deprive the novel of some of its dramatic quality—a man's exposure to a final and irrevocable decision and its consequences is avoided. The disillusioning thing is not that there is a plan but that the actors occasionally know the plan: that they see themselves as only God could see them —God or the novelist. *Or* the novelist? The oneness in which the two merge is no *unio mystica* but a literary knowingness, a consciousness in excess of story. Jacob's loss of Rachel is precisely so moving because it is unaccompanied by any literary theodicy, his sorrow is left unassuaged by any knowledge of what happens next; here at all events the hands that cover the weeping eyes are firmly clenched. Of course, the results of this sophisticated anticipatory device are by no means always barren. Even the scene when Joseph is thrown into the well by his exasperated brothers, his terror duly diminished by his curiosity about what will happen next, is not without its charm. But then, Joseph need not experience the fullest rigor of despair, for he will not ultimately be the one chosen from among them. But what of the others? Who is there that would carry the theme of existential and spiritual care, the sign of the election, to the end, undistracted by a sense of *déjà-vu?* Who is there to take the leap into faith, unknowing? Who will say with Job, "He is of one mind, and who can turn Him? And what His soul desireth, even that He doeth"? Even Abraham, ready to sacrifice Isaac, knows in his heart of hearts that all will be well. What God, who is not a novelist, do they all believe in?

There is, it seems to me, a connection between the two

encompassing themes, the existential and the literary. Leitmotif, irony, anticipation, Freudian analysis and Jungian typology are all designed to take the sting of finality out of experience, to make it repeatable. But in this habitual avoidance of the shocks of immediate and final experience Thomas Mann is apt to jeopardize the ultimate motivation of the whole—apt to replace religious faith by a literary faith, a sort of "pan-literariness." What I have called the existential is here a spiritual effort that receives its validation not from a goal, not from something it strives for, but from its own intensity, from within itself; a means comes to figure as an end. But since (shades of Nietzsche's Eternal Recurrence) there is no further goal, the effort, which is a conscious one, can only contemplate itself. And thus the lives of the main characters appear, to us *and* to themselves, as parts of a fully determined plan, that is, as an aesthetic spectacle.

The connection that emerges between the two themes is of the kind that Rilke had in mind when he wrote of "the many-digited sum that turns into zero," or when he described that place in experience where "pure want" ("das reine Zuwenig") topples over into "empty excess" ("jenes leere Zuviel"). But Thomas Mann does not see it in this way. He does not appear to heed the disillusioning effect of his device, the disabling literariness of his idea of God. In calling this device disabling one is not advancing any theory of the ineffable; there are ages when poets have written unembarrassedly about God and His design with men. But there are situations which, though not beyond the power of language to describe, are certainly beyond the scope of that literary self-consciousness to which Mann so readily resorts. And one need be no theologian to conclude that, whatever it is that constitutes an enrichment of the laconic story of Genesis, it is not Mann's idea of God, the encompassing motivation of his novel.

"The greatest achievement of the greatest living man of

letters" the late Ernest Newman called *Doctor Faustus* (1947); it is certainly Mann's strangest and most powerful novel. If *Joseph and His Brothers* marks the furthest point from "the German question" at which his imagination can operate (and we have seen that even there the motivation hinges on twentieth-century concerns), with this "Life of the Composer Adrian Leverkühn, as Told by a Friend," Mann returns to the fountainhead of his inspiration and travail. How emphatically German a work this fictional biography is may be gauged from the hostility of the German critics, who found it offensive to their patriotic sense. In their polemics they have turned against the symbolical intention of the work, condemning the fundamental disproportion (as they see it) between the life depicted and the criticism of Germany intimated through that life. The fate of a single man, the drama of a solitary, desolate soul (they have argued) cannot be made to "stand for" the fate of a whole nation—not without overstraining the resources of narrative art and doing scant justice to history. The criticism is not unfounded. The signs of strain are certainly there. (In the autobiographical *Genesis of Doctor Faustus*, 1949, Mann tells us that the writing of the novel undermined his health and almost broke his spirit.) The discursiveness of some chapters, the variety of narrative devices and complex mixing of levels of action, the indulgence in all sorts of technicalities, the profusion of anecdotes and occasional looseness of structure—all these suggest a work written at the point of the utmost spiritual and imaginative exertion, and occasionally beyond it. And the equation of man and history—Leverkühn and Germany in the first forty years of this century—*is* in some ways lopsided. To put it in generic terms, the novel does belong among those "baggy monsters" of German literature from Goethe's *Faust II* onwards, in which something like a total vision of man is attempted. Yet a reader of Thomas Mann will at all times do well to moderate his appetite for "symbolical" parallels; his

[35]

first attention should be to the personal story the work offers.

Its subject matter is the life and times of a major modern composer (the German subtitle uses the archaic "Tonsetzer"), from his birth in 1885 in a small town in Central Germany, through his school days, university studies, his working years in Munich and on a Bavarian farm, to his illness, mental collapse in 1930, and, finally, his death in 1940. The story is told by one Serenus Zeitblom, D.Phil., Adrian Leverkühn's lifelong friend and companion. Through the urbane, circumstantial, and pedantic pen of Studienrat Zeitblom—a classical philologist and amateur musician—Mann once again imparts meaningful form to a vast and potentially inchoate subject matter. The sources on which he draws for the background and various episodes of Leverkühn's life include the writings of Luther and the German Reformation, an early Faust chapbook and Goethe's drama; they range from Gogol's diaries and Ivan Karamazov's conversation with the Devil to Nietzsche's letters, studies of Beethoven, Tchaikovsky, Hugo Wolf, and Schönberg; there are motifs from Ernest Newman's Wagner biography, Richard Strauss, Gustav Mahler, and Kierkegaard's *Either/Or;* Wilhelminian nationalists, Spenglerians, and the racialists of the twenties appear on the scene; salient points in the history of Germany, from the early years of the century to the Allied bombing of "Festung Europa" in the forties, are retraced in terms of individual lives; botany, organic chemistry, alchemy, as well as musical theory and philosophical speculation, provide much of the symbolism: the instrumentation of this biography in the grand manner is indeed complex and abundant.

The central experience of Leverkühn's life is his solitude. Is it caused by his musical precocity and genius? Or are these the consolations of a proud and aloof mind? Is the disease he knowingly contracts the price of his musical gift, the cause of his lonely distinction? Is the pact he signs with an icy hyperborean

[36]

Devil (who speaks the language of Luther's visitor on the Wartburg) the means which secure him further creative inspiration? Yet they but confirm the underlying conviction that Leverkühn's election for greatness is inseparable from his election for tragic solitude.

A rich panorama of life, most of it seen through the eyes of Zeitblom, is evoked round Adrian. The friendships he attempts, the love affair that comes to nothing, the several circles and cliques that form round him, the family ties that are interposed between him and his fate—all the ingredients of the realistic novel are here. But (and this is one of the novel's triumphs) the social realism is there not in order to round out and give substance to Adrian's life but on the contrary to set off the core of the novel—which is the single, solitary man, infinitely moving in his proud, chilly isolation, the bearer of a gift that destroys him. It is not the purchase of that gift from the Devil (at a time when his "natural" inspiration is about to peter out) that is Adrian's ultimate impiety. The guilt of hubris which is inseparable from his creativeness is not a moral guilt but a disposition of mind, the sign not of riches but of deprivation. And a deprivation so radical and so destructive of life in Adrian and around him—that, certainly, is a theme in the grand manner. What was said earlier about Mann's excessive readiness to cushion the shocks of experience no longer applies here. The crowning achievement of the novel is the strange charm—a charm that belongs to every tragic hero in literature—which lies like an aura round the solitary Leverkühn, not diminishing but heightening the poignancy of his fate.

Solitude is not a theme commonly found in European fiction, but it is emphatically a German theme. Furthermore, it is significant that Adrian is a composer, that he writes a work which is intended to "take back" Beethoven's Ninth Symphony (as his life "takes back" the life of Goethe's Faust). Thus there is a

[37]

sense in which it is not fanciful to see it as something like a
musical theme—one thinks of the isolation of the human voice
from the orchestration in Schönberg's *Pierrot lunaire* and Alban
Berg's *Wozzeck.* Mann's task, we can now see, is complex: not
only must he transpose a musician's work and thinking about
his work into words, but Leverkühn's whole mode of life as a
musician and as a solitary requires this kind of transposing.
Adrian's desolation of soul is as absolute as a novel involved in
social circumstance can make it. Indeed, *Doctor Faustus* may
well stand as the measure of the theme in world literature.

The penultimate chapter of the novel takes place on a farm
not far from Munich where Leverkühn, now about to succumb
to paralysis of the insane, has been living in retirement. In a
moment of euphoria he has invited a large number of acquaint-
ances, musical critics, writers, singers, and cultural busybodies,
to tell them of his latest composition, *Doctor Fausti Lament,*
and to play to them piano excerpts from it; the invitation, the
anxious Zeitblom tells us, is wholly uncharacteristic. The scene
that ensues in the large hall of the ancient Bavarian farmhouse is
carefully set in several contrasting moods. Humorous, even
ribald effects are derived from the contrast between the with-
drawn unworldliness and inward concentration of the host,
Adrian Leverkühn, and the various visitors: some blasé and
sophisticated, others hoping for a sensation and indulging in the
scandalous nature of the occasion, some affectionate and fearful
of the outcome, others pompously conscious of the "historic
moment." But there is no danger that these humorous openings
will impair the tragic climax. Only the last sentence that Leverkühn addresses to his worldly audience is concerned with the
choral-symphonic work which he has just completed. The
long, all but incoherent yet meaningful speech which, to their
growing embarrassment, he delivers is his life's confession. In
that strange German full of Lutheran archaisms and idio-

[38]

syncratic turns which he affects in his demented stage he tells them of the impious origin of his inspiration and work, his transactons with the Devil, his cold pride and despairing solitude, and his terror of the damnation of his soul. He is demented. Clearly, all the visitors think him so; even the solicitous Zeitblom, it appears, whose heart bleeds for his friend, believes that Adrian's confession and searing self-accusations are insane. Is Marlowe's Faustus insane? Is that last great speech of his no more than a monstrous psychotic delusion? Certainly Thomas Mann has provided the grounds for a detailed psychosomatic explanation; accordingly, the story of the conversation with the Devil and many similar episodes of a supernatural kind may be seen as mere devices to dramatize a pathological delusion. Yet even so the tragedy of the modern Doctor Faustus retains a spiritual and religious meaning. If we accept Leverkühn's own account of his deliberate contracting of the disease that eventually leads to his insanity as objectively true, then his sin of spiritual pride and its punishment must be given the same status. This account also, it is true, is viewed by some of the characters in the light of psychological explanation, as a delusion; and so we trace the disease further back still, to Adrian's boyhood and the congenital migraine from which he suffered. . . . But however far back we go in the history of the man, there always remains an element of spiritual-religious motivation which eludes the causal accounts of psychology or medicine. If Thomas Mann can present the religious element in no other way than as an asymptotic line that comes ever closer to a psychological explanation yet is never quite coincident with it, then that, once again, is a sign of his dialectical truthfulness. Spirituality is acknowledged against the greatest odds that his imagination can devise.

Yet (to return to our earlier argument) *Doctor Faustus* cannot be read exclusively in terms of a personal history. Germany is *in* the novel—it is in Adrian's blood, and in Zeitblom's. Her otherworldliness and bellicosity, her metaphysics and paroxysms of hysteria, her provincialism and grand airs, her humanity and inhumanities, her solitude and music—they are all present as both background to and aspects of Adrian's own life. This complex reciprocity between life and times is to be found throughout the novel; a telling example of it is provided by Mann's account of Leverkühn's last and greatest musical composition. The state of mind in which he purchases his inspiration from the Devil is one of exhaustion. What is exhausted is not only Adrian's creative vein but (as he sees it) the musical tradition in which he was reared; it is as though all possible, possibly valid changes had been rung, and "natural" inspiration could invent no new ones. Before him lies anarchy, the license to do anything, anything at all, in order to avoid the banal and derivative—a false freedom which settles "like mildew" upon the soul. The inspiration he buys in this predicament vouchsafes him an escape from compositional sterility *and* personal isolation, an escape into "polyphonic objectivity," that is, a music (a state of mind, an ideology) which replaces the "mildew freedom" of the individual by "the choral discipline of the collective." In this vicarious way Adrian's solitary soul attempts to grapple itself to humanity: by exchanging an unmanageable personal freedom for the assurance of discipline and regimentation, by escaping from a desolate subjectivity into conformity with the "objective forces of history." And the readiness for just such a diabolical exchange (as Erich Heller has pointed out) was among the major causes of the undoing of Germany in our time. Occasionally, it is true, the historical parallels (like the theological speculations in the *Joseph* novel) threaten to overwhelm the story. But if we avoid literal-mindedness (that most comic of vices, no longer a German prerogative) we shall find the balance reestablished at all salient points of the novel:

[40]

the balance, that is, between the solitary man and his time and country of desolation.

The genealogy of *Confessions of Felix Krull* is indicative of the remarkable coherence of Thomas Mann's inspiration. Begun in 1909, the first five chapters of these memoirs of a confidence man were published as a fragment in 1922; the novel's first and only volume was completed in 1954, without any alterations and in the same tone as the early fragment. The voluble first-person tale of this amiable sharper in the Edwardian Europe of luxury hotels, grand titles, and grand passions, full of ribald episodes and stylistic spoofs, is above all things an act of liberation, for its creator as much as for his readers. The literary parody harks back to the picaresque novels of the seventeenth century yet the narrator's disclosures, at once outrageous and urbane, seedy and comic, belong to the world of Krueger, Stavisky, and Sacha Guitry. Krull is a virtuoso in the medium of life and a servant of Hermes, god of thieves. His story demythologizes Joseph's life in Egypt and parodies his immense successes among its high society. The mode is occasionally satirical, as in the superb scene when the young Felix avoids conscription into the German Imperial Army by feigning an attack of epilepsy, his convulsions rendered the more convincing by his protestations of eagerness to do his patriotic duty. But the satire is mild, the comic muse left untrammeled. In many of his earlier novels Mann had given reign to his love of descriptive detail. Here a glittering parade of exquisite pieces of jewelry, magnificent shop windows and hotel interiors, all faithful to their age of luxury and precarious stability, passes before our eyes. An old man's peroration on the riches that furnished the world of his youth? Yet the gaiety and humor are untainted by any nostalgia except the hero's; and he has good reason for being nostalgic, seeing that he composes his memoirs in prison.

Once again the use to which Mann puts an elaborate social realism is characteristically his own: whereas in *Doctor Faustus* it served to set off the central figure in its tragic solitude, here the very solidity of the world of material things and social classes, the rotund phraseology and fine manners, are evoked to show how easily this world may be conquered and exploited by a young man with good looks, a quick intelligence, and an almost infinite adaptability. A charming ease: in manner and thought, in speech and amorous intercourse, in learning to play tennis or listening to a learned discourse on the origin of the species—a charming ease is Felix Krull's device in life. In another world it might amount to a grace. But here, once again, it is parody, a guying of Thomas Mann's own lifelong concern with the strenuous deliverance of man: on that validation too Krull's easy conscience offers a last ironical comment. An act of liberation penned by a jailbird? The novel remains unfinished; we don't know which of Krull's adventures landed him behind bars. But Thomas Mann would not be ineluctably German were he not to believe, with his dubious hero, that "to live in true freedom is to live symbolically," that is, in the spirit.

In concentrating on the more difficult of Thomas Mann's works many other amiable divertissements have had to be omitted. Chief among these is *Royal Highness* (1909), a story of princely initiation told in the easy style of an ironic fairy tale for grown-ups. The young ruling prince of an imaginary kingdom on the verge of bankruptcy, his exotic and extravagantly rich bride, and her American millionaire father form a charade of characters that might belong to a gay *Golden Bowl* without any of its moral problems; Prince Klaus Heinrich's tutor, on the other hand, the passionate intellectual Dr. Raoul Überbein, anticipates the fanatical Naphta of *The Magic Mountain* before Georg Lukács, its real-life prototype, had ever crossed Thomas Mann's path.

[42]

My list of omissions is embarrassingly long. It includes Mann's numerous literary essays, among the finest of them his studies of Freud (1936), Wagner (1937), Chekhov (1954), and Schiller (1955); it also includes *Lotte in Weimar* (written in 1939, between the third and fourth volumes of the *Joseph* novel), a tour de force of literary and biographical reconstruction of a few days in Goethe's life in 1816, truthful to the ironic aspect of the "sage of Weimar" and to Goethe's critical attitude to the Germany of his time. The interest of these works is never undivided. They certainly illuminate their respective subject matters, and as such they also contain sketches for a portrait of the artist and intellectual in our time. Finally, I have also omitted some slighter works, mainly of Mann's last decade, in which the dialectics of knowingness are carried to the point of tedium.

The difficulty, then, on which I have concentrated is in the first instance a matter of Mann's literary styles. Hardly ever simple and direct, informed by a variety of allusions and parodistic devices, they have a fatal tendency to be reduced in English translations to a single, regrettable level of archness. The novel, for Thomas Mann, is neither a verbal icon nor social reportage, though it includes elements of both. The syntactic finesses, stylistic impersonations, and quotational devices serve not a single point of view but a complex mode of indirection. The aim is rational insight issuing in high intellectual delight; and through its chinks we occasionally glimpse an impenetrable solitude. Impenetrable because no longer subject to any dialectic, this solitude constitutes, for Mann, the ground of the being of modern man.

The impression we are thus left with is one of an immense narrative ease which now intimates now conceals that idea of the strenuous deliverance and validation of man to which the author returns throughout the six decades of faithful devotion

[43]

to his métier. Of this idea and mode of life *Doctor Faustus* is the final and greatest embodiment. The religious dimension of Adrian Leverkühn's life (we have seen) is acknowledged against the greatest odds the novelist's imagination and truthfulness can devise; but even this is not the whole story. What is acknowledged is, more problematically still, not God but "that highly religious person," the Devil. Serenus Zeitblom believes that Leverkühn will be saved. But that salvation (he tells us) can only come at the price of despair, the despair Adrian voices in his last speech:

Perchance also God seeth that I sought the hard travail and labored with might and main [dass ich das Schwere gesucht und mirs habe sauer werden lassen], perchance, perchance it will unto my credit accrue and be added unto me that I so applied myself and all things strenuously completed—but I cannot say and have not courage to hope

for, as the poet says, "hope would be hope for the wrong thing." Beyond this cloud of unknowing Thomas Mann cannot go. Whenever he tries to penetrate it, a disillusioning knowingness takes over. But here, beneath the cloud, speaks one of the authentic voices of our age. And in his commitment to that age, not despite it, lies his claim upon the attention of posterity. In *Death in Venice* he defines the grounds on which fame—his fame, at all events—is likely to rest:

A significant creation of the mind [he writes there] can only then yield an immediate influence which shall also be deep and lasting if it is founded in a secret affinity and consonance between the personal destiny of its author and the destiny of his contemporaries in general. Men do not know why they bestow fame on a work of art. . . . The true ground of their commendation is an imponderable: it is sympathy.

[44]

SELECTED BIBLIOGRAPHY

NOTE: *Thomas Mann's happy association with the publisher Samuel Fischer began in 1898, and culminated in the publication of Mann's collected works in 12 vols., S. Fischer Verlag, Frankfurt/M., 1960 f., to which further volumes of letters and posthumous papers are being added. Another collected edition, by the East German Aufbau Verlag, began appearing in 1956.*

The following is a list of translations of Mann's major works; unless otherwise stated, the translator is the late Mrs. H. T. Lowe-Porter, and the publishers Alfred A. Knopf, New York; the dates are those of first American editions, not of the numerous reprints.

PRINCIPAL WORKS OF THOMAS MANN

Buddenbrooks. 1924.

Death in Venice. Tr. Kenneth Burke, 1925. Another tr. by Mrs. Lowe-Porter, 1930.

Royal Highness. Tr. A. C. Curtis, 1926; tr. Mrs. Lowe-Porter, 1939; revised by C. McCab in "New English Library," London, 1962.

The Magic Mountain. 1927.

Children and Fools. Tr. H. G. Scheffauer, 1928. (Includes the early [1898] story, "Little Herr Friedemann.")

Three Essays [includes "Goethe and Tolstoy" and "Frederick the Great and the Grand Coalition"]. 1929.

Early Sorrow. Tr. H. G. Scheffauer, 1930.

Mario and the Magician. 1931.

Past Masters and Other Papers. 1933.

Joseph and His Brothers [i.e., Die Geschichten Jaakobs], 1934; Young Joseph, 1935; Joseph in Egypt, 1938; Joseph the Provider, 1944.

Stories of Three Decades. 1936.

Freud, Goethe, Wagner [Essays]. 1937.

The Beloved Returns: Lotte in Weimar. 1940.

The Transposed Heads: A Legend of India. 1941.

Order of the Day: Political Essays and Speeches of Two Decades. 1942.

The Tables of the Law [i.e., Das Gesetz]. 1945.

Doctor Faustus: The Life of the German Composer, Adrian Leverkühn, as Told by a Friend. 1948.

The Holy Sinner [i.e., Der Erwählte]. 1951.

The Black Swan [i.e., Die Betrogene]. Tr. W. R. Trask. London, Secker & Warburg, 1954.

[45]

Confessions of Felix Krull, Confidence Man: The Early Years. Tr. Denver Lindley, 1955.
Last Essays. Tr. C. Winston and T. and J. Stern, 1959.
A Sketch of My Life. 1960.
Letters to Paul Amann, 1915–1952. Ed. H. Wegener, tr. R. and C. Winston. Middletown, Conn., Wesleyan University Press, 1960.
The Story of a Novel: The Genesis of Doctor Faustus. Tr. R. and C. Winston. London, Secker & Warburg, 1961.

CRITICAL WORKS AND COMMENTARY

Bauer, A. Thomas Mann und die Krise.der bürgerlichen Kultur in Deutschland. Berlin, 1946.
Bergsten, G. Thomas Manns "Doktor Faustus": Untersuchungen zu den Quellen und zur Struktur des Romans. Stockholm, 1963.
Bertram, E. "Thomas Manns *Betrachtungen eines Unpolitischen,*" *Mitteilungen der literarhistorischen Gesellschaft in Bonn,* Vol. XX, 1917.
Blackmur, R. P. "Hans Castorp, Small Lord of the Counterpositions," *Hudson Review,* Vol. I, 1948.
Blume, B. Thomas Mann und Goethe. Berne, 1949.
Brennan, J. G. Three Philosophical Novelists: James Joyce, André Gide, Thomas Mann. New York, 1964.
Bürgin, H. Das Werk Thomas Manns: Eine Bibliographie . . . Frankfurt/M., 1959.
Bürgin, H., and H.-O. Mayer. Thomas Mann: Eine Chronik seines Lebens. Frankfurt/M., 1965.
Cassirer, E. "Thomas Manns Goethe-Bild: Eine Studie über *Lotte in Weimar,*" *Germanic Review,* Vol. XX, 1945.
Eichner, H. Thomas Mann: Eine Einführung in sein Werk. Berne, 1953.
Eloesser, A. Thomas Mann. Berlin, 1925.
Faesi, R. Thomas Mann, ein Meister der Erzählkunst. Zurich, 1955.
Flinker, M. Thomas Manns politische Betrachtungen im Lichte der heutigen Zeit. The Hague, 1959.
Fougère, J. Thomas Mann, ou la séduction de la mort. Paris, 1947.
Fourrier, G. Thomas Mann: Le message d'un artiste-bourgeois, 1896–1924. Paris, 1960.
Gray, R. D. The German Tradition in Literature, 1871–1945. Cambridge, 1965. Part 2.
Hamburger, K. Thomas Mann und die Romantik. Berlin, 1932.
—— Thomas Manns Roman "Joseph und seine Brüder." Stockholm, 1945.

[46]

Hamburger, M. From Prophecy to Exorcism. London, 1965. Chapter 4.

Hatfield, H. Thomas Mann: An Introduction to His Fiction. London, 1952.

Hatfield, H., ed. Thomas Mann: A Collection of Critical Essays. Englewood Cliffs, N.J., 1964.

Heller, E. The Ironic German: A Study of Thomas Mann. New York, 1958.

Heller, P. Dialectics and Nihilism. Amherst, Mass., 1966. Part 3.

Hirschbach, F. D. The Arrow and the Lyre: A Study of the Role of Love in the Works of Thomas Mann. The Hague, 1955.

Hofmiller, J. "Thomas Manns neue Erzählung ['Der [Tod in Venedig'],″ Süddeutsche Monatshefte, Vol. X, 1913.

Holthusen, H.-E. Die Welt ohne Transzendenz. Hamburg, 1949.

Jonas, K. W. Fifty Years of Thomas Mann Studies: A Bibliography of Criticism. Minneapolis, 1955.

Kaufmann, F. L. Thomas Mann: The World as Will and Representation. Boston, 1957.

Keller, E. Der unpolitische Deutsche: Eine Studie zu den "Betrachtungen eines Unpolitischen." Berne, 1965.

Kerenyi, K. Romandichtung und Mythologie: Ein Briefwechsel mit Thomas Mann. Zurich, 1945.

Lesser, J. Thomas Mann in der Epoche seiner Vollendung. Munich, 1952.

Lindsay, J. M. Thomas Mann. Oxford, 1955.

Lukács, G. Die Theorie des Romans. Berlin, 1920/1963.

—— Thomas Mann. Berlin, 1949/1957.

—— Wider den missverstandenen Realismus. Berlin, 1958.

Mann, V. Wir waren fünf. Constance, 1949.

Mayer, H. Thomas Mann: Werk und Entwicklung. Berlin, 1950.

Muschg, W. Tragische Literaturgeschichte. Berne, 1948.

Neider, C., ed. The Stature of Thomas Mann. New York, 1947.

Pascal, R. The German Novel. Manchester, 1956. Chapter 9.

Peacock, R. Das Leitmotiv bei Thomas Mann. Berne, 1934.

Samuel, R. H. "Thomas Mann und Hans Grimm," German Life and Letters, January, 1937.

Schaukal, R. [Review of] "Der kleine Herr Friedemann," Die Gesellschaft, Vol. XIV, 1895.

Schröter, K. Thomas Mann. Hamburg [Rowohlts monographien], 1964.

Seidlin, O. Von Goethe zu Thomas Mann. Göttingen, 1963.

Sontheimer, K. Thomas Mann und die Deutschen. Munich, 1961.

[47]

Staiger, E. "Thomas Manns *Doktor Faustus*," *Neue Schweizer Rundschau*, November, 1947.

Thomas, R. H. Thomas Mann: The Mediation of Art. Oxford, 1956.

Weigand, H. J. Thomas Mann's Novel "Der Zauberberg." New York, 1933; Chapel Hill, 1964.

Wenzel, G., ed. Vollendung und Grösse Thomas Manns: Beiträge zu Werk und Persönlichkeit des Dichters. Halle/S., 1962.

White, A. Thomas Mann. Edinburgh, 1965.

Wilkinson, E. M. [Introduction to ed. of] "Tonio Kröger." Oxford, 1946.